Bon Voyage!

by SCHULZ

HarperCollinsPublishers

Happy Trails!

ALL PACKED, HUH?

WELL, YOU'LL HAVE A GOOD TIME...

IF YOU GET A CHANCE, SEND ME A POSTCARD

SO LONG, LITTLE FRIEND...

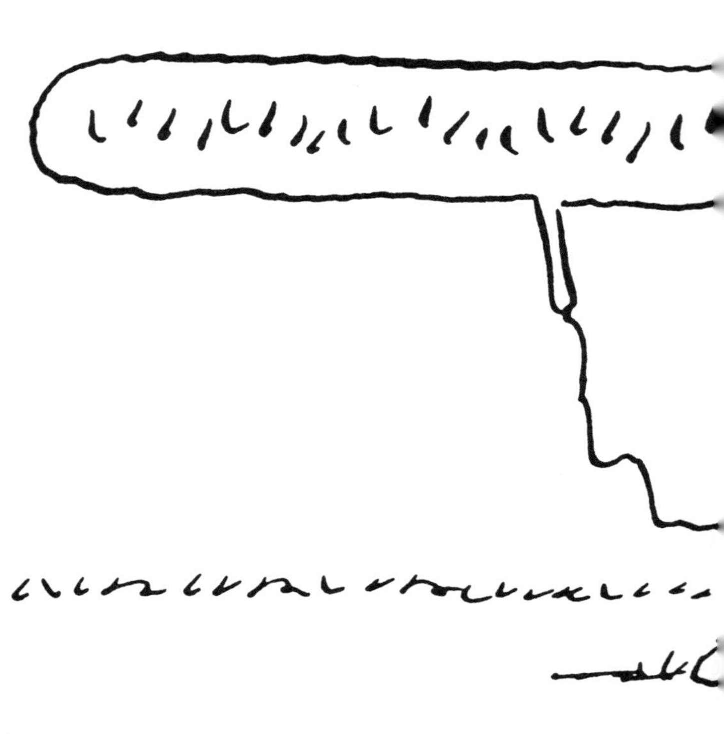

I HATE LONG GOODBYES

SURE, WHY NOT?

NOW WOULD BE A GOOD TIME BECAUSE MOST OF THE TOURISTS WILL BE GONE..

THE WATER IS STILL WARM, TOO...

YOU CAN SIT UNDER A BIG UMBRELLA, AND READ A BOOK AND LISTEN TO YOUR TAPES... IT'LL BE GOOD FOR YOU!

HAVE A NICE TRIP...SEND ME A POSTCARD

Don't Forget To Write!

Dear Marcie and Chuck,
Well, your ol' friend
Patty is here in Paris.

You know what we eat here for breakfast? Bread and hot chocolate!
Here is a photograph of me with a loaf of French bread.

And here is a picture of me dunking my bread in the hot chocolate.

Dear Marcie,
I am still having a
good time here in Paris.

We just had lunch
in a very nice
little restaurant.

You'd be proud of me. I'm learning to order in French.

GARÇON, JUNK FOOD, S'IL VOUS PLAÎT!

KNOCK KNOCK
?

HI, MARCIE! I'M BACK FROM PARIS!

CLICK!

CLICK!

CLICK!

SIR, I DON'T WANT TO LOOK AT YOUR VACATION PICTURES AT THREE O'CLOCK IN THE MORNING!

I HAVE JET LAG, MARCIE.. I CAN'T SLEEP...I'M STILL ON PARIS TIME... I'M READY FOR LUNCH...

GOOD NIGHT, SIR
PEANUT BUTTER ON A CROISSANT SOUNDS GOOD...

HarperCollins*Publishers*

Produced by Jennifer Barry Design, Sausalito, CA
Creative consultation by Kristen Schilo
First published in 1998 by HarperCollins*Publishers* Inc.
http://www.harpercollins.com

Based on the PEANUTS ® comic strip by Charles M. Schulz
http://www.unitedmedia.com

ISBN 0-06-107513-2

Printed in Hong Kong

1 3 5 7 9 10 8 6 4 2